Super C

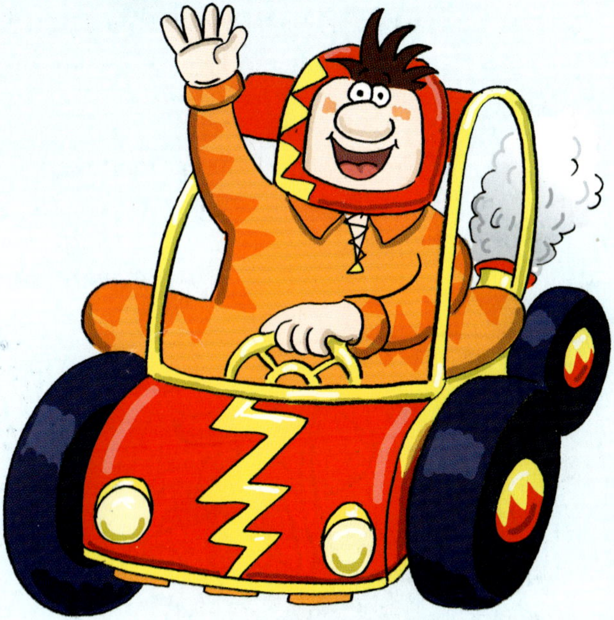

Monica Hughes
Illustrated by Lucy Maddison

RIGBY

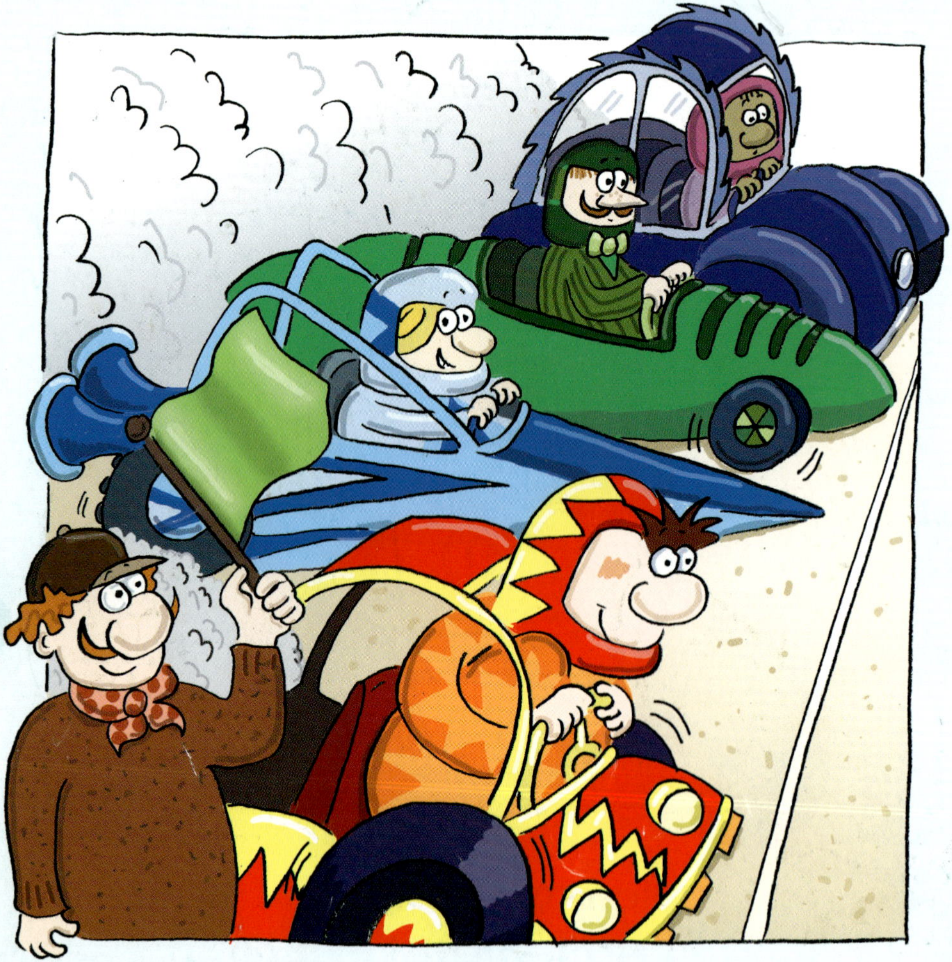

Go! Go! Go!

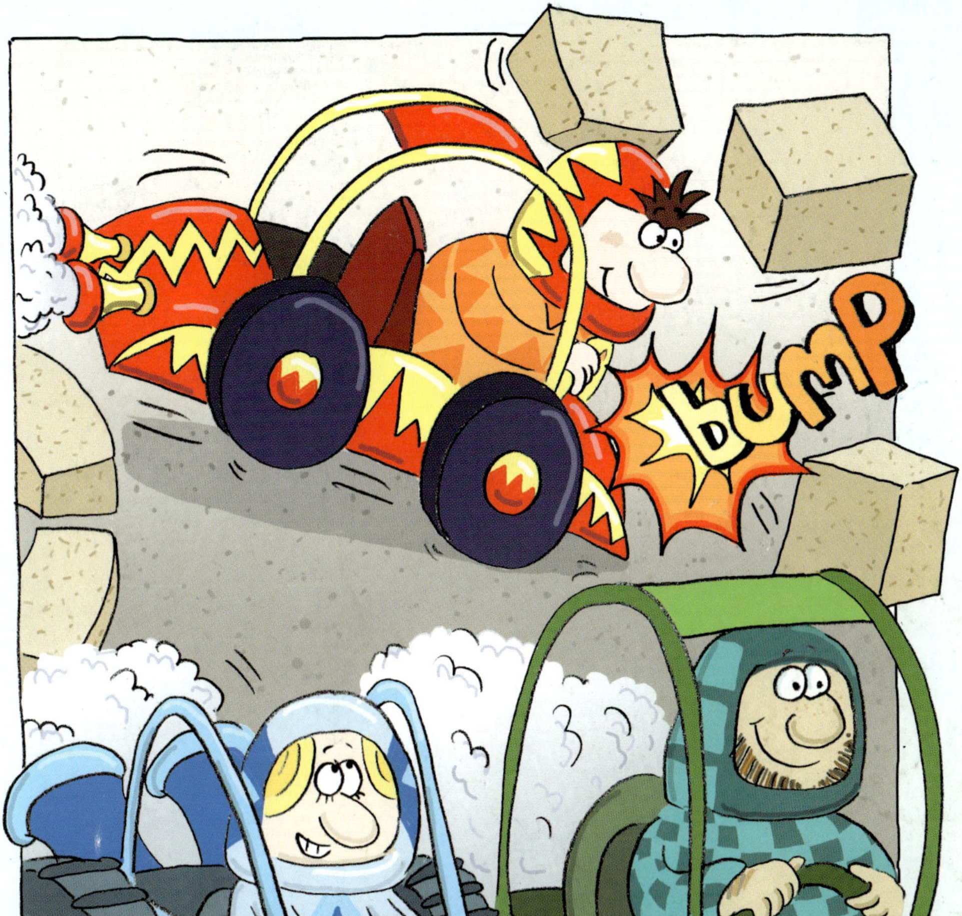

It can bump.

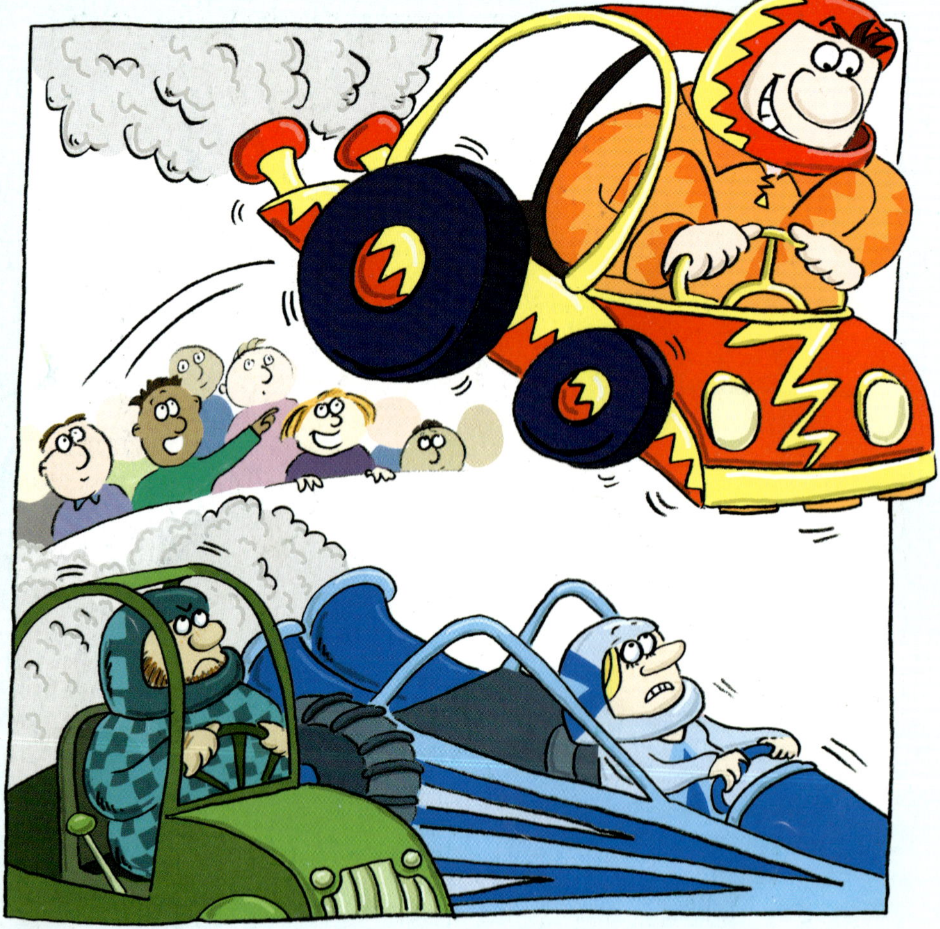

It can jump.

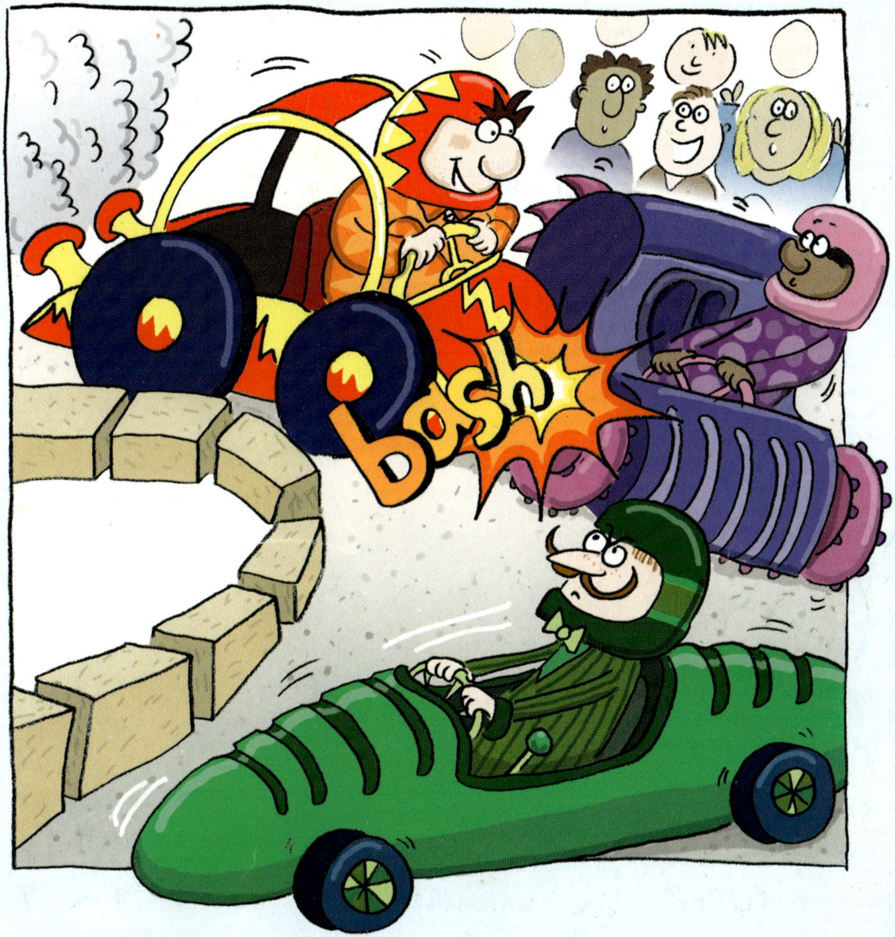

It can bash.

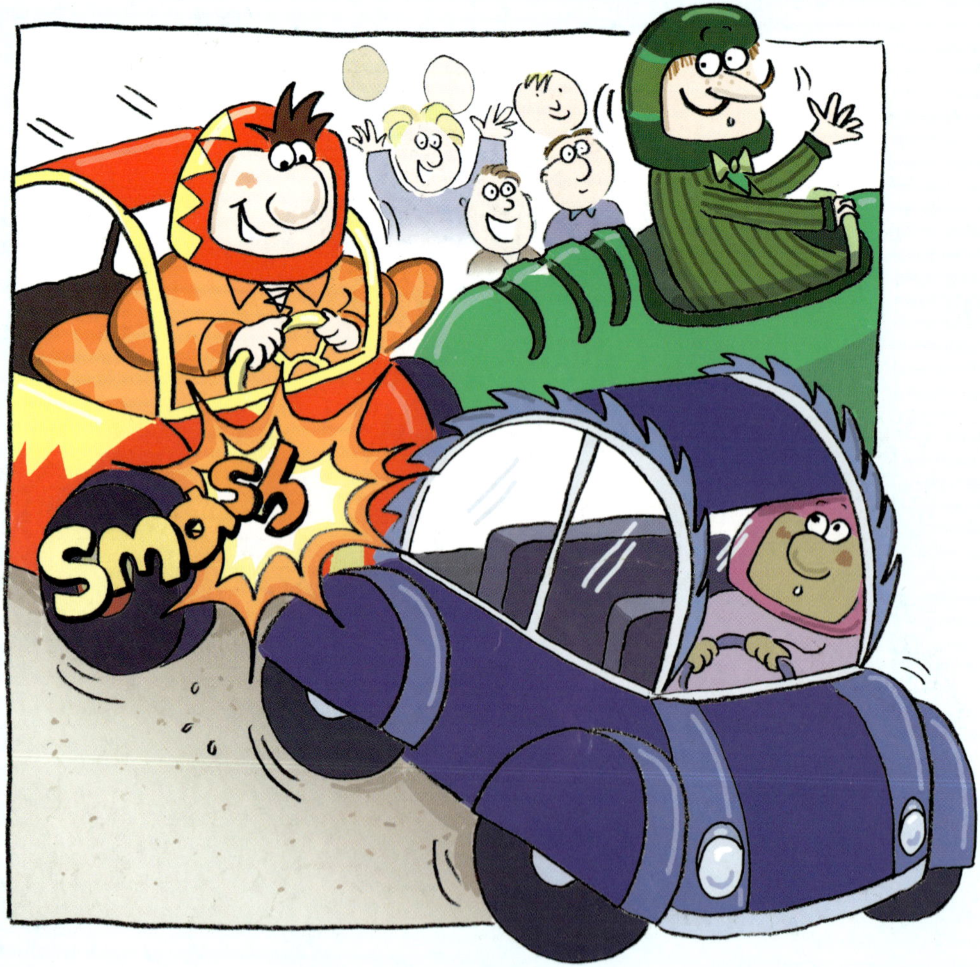

It can smash.

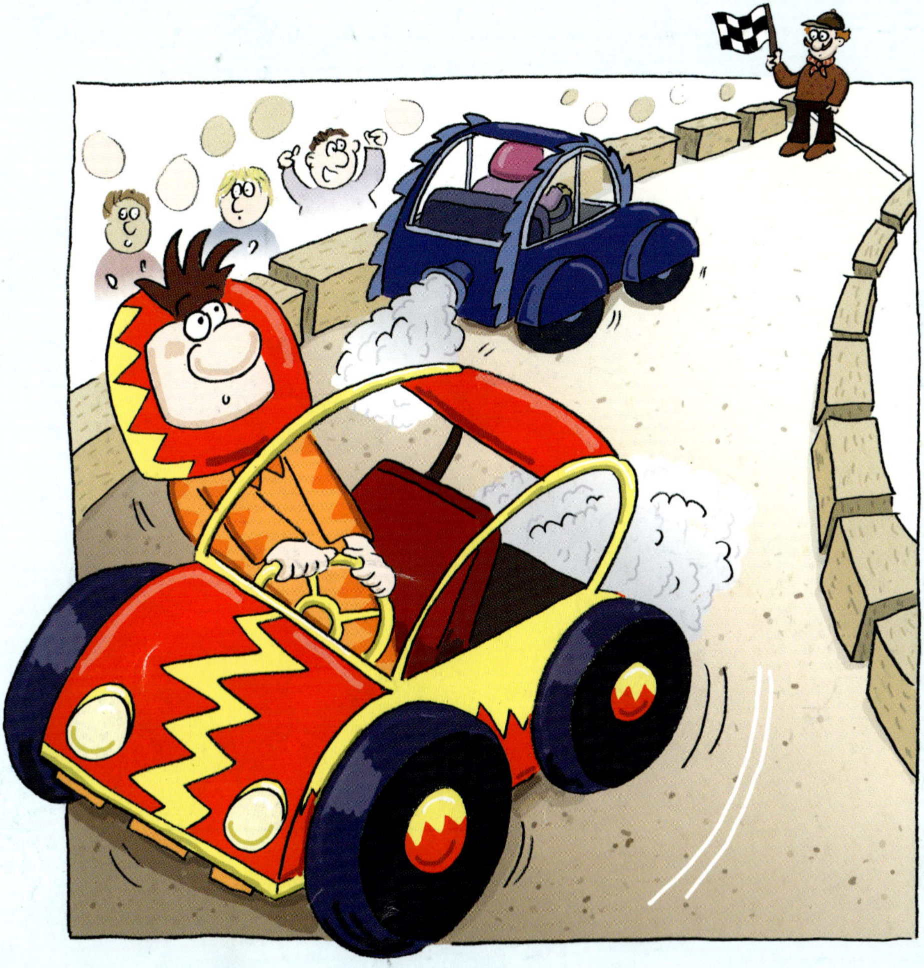

It can spin.

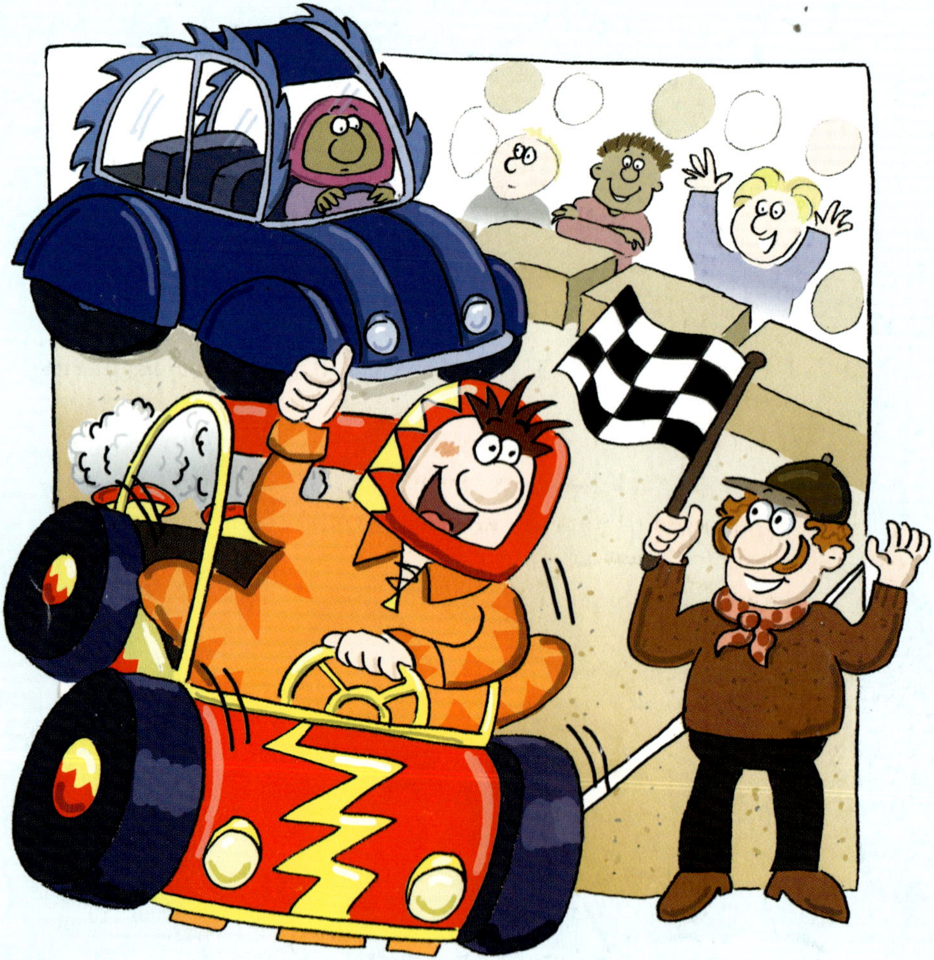

It can win!